Animal Attack and Defense

WARNING COLORS

Kimberley Jane Pryor

Marshall Cavendish
Benchmark

New York

This edition first published in 2010 in the United States of America by
MARSHALL CAVENDISH BENCHMARK.

MARSHALL CAVENDISH BENCHMARK
99 White Plains Road
Tarrytown, NY 10591
www.marshallcavendish.us

All Internet sites were available and accurate when sent to press.

First published in 2008 by
MACMILLAN EDUCATION AUSTRALIA PTY LTD
15–19 Claremont Street, South Yarra 3141

Visit our website at www.macmillan.com.au or go directly to www.macmillanlibrary.com.au

Associated companies and representatives throughout the world.

Copyright © Kimberley Jane Pryor 2009

Library of Congress Cataloging-in-Publication Data

Pryor, Kimberley Jane.
    Warning colors / by Kimberley Jane Pryor.
        p. cm. – (Animal attack and defense)
    Includes index.
    Summary: "Discusses how animals use warning colors to protect themselves from predators or to catch prey"–
Provided by publisher.
    ISBN 978-0-7614-4419-0
    1. Warning coloration (Biology)–Juvenile literature. I. Title.
    QL767.P79 2009
591.47'2–dc22
                                                                        2009004992

Edited by Julia Carlomagno
Text and cover design by Ben Galpin
Page layout by Domenic Lauricella
Photo research by Claire Armstrong and Legend Images

Printed in the United States

Acknowledgments
The author and the publisher are grateful to the following for permission to reproduce copyright material:

Cover and title page photo of a poison dart frog © Blickwinkel/Alamy/Photolibrary

Photos courtesy of: © Blickwinkel/Alamy/Photolibrary, **27**; © Nick Greaves/Alamy/Photolibrary, **22**; © David
Hosking/Alamy/Photolibrary, **18**; © WildPictures/Alamy/Photolibrary, **28**; © Willie Manalo/Dreamstime.com, **16**;
© www.flagstaffotos.com.au, **10**; © Getty Images/Michael & Patricia Fogden, **25**; © Getty Images/Mark Moffett,
4; © Getty Images/Ian Waldie, **14**; © iStockphoto.com, **12**; © Beverly Guhl Davis/iStockphoto.com, **19**; ©
Daniel Gustavsson/iStockphoto.com, **5**; © Michael Guttman/iStockphoto.com, **17**; © Laurie Knight/iStockphoto.
com, **15**; © Karel Lgm/iStockphoto.com, **20**; © Sven Peter/iStockphoto.com, **7**; © Klemens Wolf/iStockphoto.
com, **30** (right); Photolibrary/Erwin & Peggy Bauer, **9**; Photolibrary/Joseph T Collins, **6**; Photolibrary/Creatas,
24; Photolibrary/Michael Fogden, **29**; Photolibrary/Paul Freed, **21**; Photolibrary/Patti Murray, **13**; Photolibrary/
James H Robinson, **23**; Photos.com, **11**; © Tomasz Pietryszek/Shutterstock, **30** (left); © Greg Wallis, **8**; Wikimedia
Commons/Jens Petersen, **26**.

For Nick, Ashley, and Thomas

1 3 5 6 4 2

Contents

Glossary Word

When a word is printed in **bold**, you can look up its meaning in the glossary on page 31.

Warning Colors..........

A slug caterpillar's bright colors warn predators to keep away from its spines.

Types of Warning Colors

The most common warning colors are colors that can be seen easily, such as red and yellow. Animals often have two or more warning colors. Sometimes bright colors are **combined** with brown or black. Sometimes warning colors form patterns, such as spots or stripes. Some dangerous animals have a small patch of bright color, and some are brightly colored all over.

How Warning Colors Protect Animals

Warning colors protect animals from predators. Animals with warning colors do not need to hide or run away from predators in their **habitats**. They are not often attacked because predators avoid them.

A predator that tries to eat a bad-tasting or poisonous animal will not want to do it again. It will remember the bright colors and patterns of the animal and avoid it in the future. This way, neither the predator nor its **prey**, the colorful animal, will be harmed.

The pink dorid is a sea slug whose bright colors warn predators that it tastes bad.

Coral Snakes

A Coral Snake's Colorful Patterns

In North America, coral snakes with red bands next to yellow bands are venomous.

Coral snakes are beautiful but dangerous. Their red, black, and yellow bands warn other animals that they produce very powerful **venom**.

Coral snakes are hardly ever seen. They hide under the ground and in thick leaf litter on the forest floor. When coral snakes bite, they hold onto victims with their fangs and release venom into the wounds.

The bright colors of the eastern coral snake warn predators that it is venomous.

Colorful patterns are often seen on animals that are **venomous**, or **poisonous** when eaten.

A garden tiger moth has colorful patterns to warn predators that it is poisonous.

Vital Statistics

- **Wingspan:** up to 2.6 inches (65 millimeters)
- **Habitat:** dandelion, stinging nettle, and bramble plants
- **Distribution:** Europe, Asia, and North America
- **Predators:** spiders, frogs, birds, and bats

Garden Tiger Moths

Garden tiger moths fly around at night. Their colorful **hind wings** warn other animals that they are poisonous.

A garden tiger moth caterpillar nibbles on all kinds of soft green plants that grow close to the ground. It takes in and stores different types of poisons from the plants. It becomes poisonous to predators, and stays poisonous when it changes into a moth.

A Garden Tiger Moth's Colorful Patterns

The front wings of a garden tiger moth are brown and white. The hind wings are orange with black spots.

7

Vital Statistics

- **Length:** 8.2 ft (2.5 meters)
- **Habitat:** forests, woodlands, swamps, and river banks
- **Distribution:** Australia
- **Predators:** other snakes

A Red-Bellied Black Snake's Red Belly

A red-bellied black snake has a glossy black back and a red, or crimson, belly.

Red-Bellied Black Snakes

Red-bellied black snakes are dangerous. Their bright red bellies tell predators that they produce deadly venom.

A red-bellied black snake hunts for frogs in damp places. If it is provoked, it raises its upper body and hisses loudly. If this warning is ignored, a red-bellied black snake **strikes**. It delivers its venom quickly in a rapid bite. Victims need medical attention right away.

A red-bellied black snake's red belly warns predators that the snake is venomous.

Animals that are venomous or poisonous sometimes have colored bellies.

A rough-skinned newt's orange belly warns predators that the newt is poisonous.

Rough-Skinned Newts

Rough-skinned newts are among the most poisonous animals in the world. Their orange bellies warn predators that they are not safe to eat.

A rough-skinned newt blends in with its surroundings because it is brown on top. However, when it is disturbed, a rough-skinned newt tilts its head back and curls its tail up to **display** its bright orange underside. At the same time, it releases poison through its skin.

Vital Statistics

- **Length:** up to 8.7 in (22 cm)
- **Habitat:** forests, woodlands, and grasslands
- **Distribution:** North America
- **Predators:** snakes

A Rough-Skinned Newt's Orange Belly

A rough-skinned newt has a brown or brown-black back, and a bright orange or yellow belly.

Red..................

Vital Statistics

- **Length:** 0.2 to 0.8 in (6 to 20 mm)
- **Habitat:** underground nests
- **Distribution:** Australia
- **Predators:** spine-covered mammals called echidnas

A Bull Ant's Red Color

Some kinds of bull ants are bright red, with yellow or orange jaws.

Bull Ants

Bull ants have a fearsome **reputation** because of their aggressive behavior and powerful stings. Some bull ants have bright red warning colors.

Bull ants are most aggressive when their nests or their young are under threat. They rush at any intruders and grip them with their long, powerful jaws. Then they swing their **abdomens** forward and insert their stings. They sting again and again, injecting small amounts of venom each time.

Red bull ants grip their victims with their strong jaws before they sting them.

Red is a well-known signal for danger. Many dangerous animals are red all over.

Bright red Madagascan tomato frogs release thick glue if attacked, to make predators spit them out.

Vital Statistics

- **Length:** up to 3.9 in (10 cm)
- **Habitat:** shallow pools and swamps
- **Distribution:** Madagascar
- **Predators:** snakes

Madagascan Tomato Frogs

Plump Madagascan tomato frogs look just like harmless tomatoes! However, their bright red colors warn that they taste bad.

Madagascan tomato frogs feed and call at night. If they feel threatened, they **inflate** themselves with air in order to look larger. If a Madagascan tomato frog is grabbed by a predator, it releases a thick glue that sticks to the predator's mouth and eyes. The glue causes **allergic reactions** in some humans.

A Madagascan Tomato Frog's Red Color

A female Madagascan tomato frog is red with a yellow belly. She may have black spots on her throat. A male Madagascan tomato frog is smaller and duller.

11

The venomous common lionfish has red-and-white stripes.

Vital Statistics

- **Length:** about 1 ft (30 cm)
- **Habitat:** coral reefs
- **Distribution:** Indian and Pacific Oceans
- **Predators:** other fish

A Lionfish's Red Stripes

Lionfish are usually reddish in color. The stripes may be red, maroon, brown, orange, yellow, black, or white.

Lionfish

Lionfish are gorgeous but dangerous fish. Their bold red stripes warn predators of their venomous fin spines.

A lionfish uses venom to defend itself against predators, but not to kill prey. It spreads out its fins as a warning when it feels threatened. If the warning is ignored, a lionfish attacks a predator with its venomous **dorsal fin** spines. The spines cause painful puncture wounds and deliver venom into the victim.

Animals with red stripes are often venomous or poisonous.

Giant Millipedes

Giant millipedes are slow-moving animals that cannot bite or sting. Some giant millipedes have red stripes to warn predators that they release poisonous liquid.

Giant millipedes coil themselves into tight spirals to protect themselves from predators. Many giant millipedes release poisonous liquid or smelly gas through tiny openings along their bodies. The liquid causes a predator's skin and eyes to itch or hurt.

Vital Statistics

- **Length:** up to 11 in (28 cm)
- **Habitat:** rain forests
- **Distribution:** Africa, Asia, and South America
- **Predators:** frogs, birds, badgers, and shrews

A Giant Millipede's Red Stripes

Most giant millipedes are black. Some have bright red stripes and bright red legs.

Some poisonous giant millipedes are black with bold red stripes.

Black and Red.........

A venomous female redback spider is black with a red stripe on her abdomen.

Vital Statistics

- **Length:** 0.4 in (11 mm)
- **Habitat:** around buildings and trash piles
- **Distribution:** Australia
- **Predators:** other spiders

A Redback Spider's Black-and-Red Colors

A female redback spider is black with a red stripe on the top of her abdomen. She also has a red spot on the underside of her abdomen.

Redback Spiders

Redback spiders are Australia's best-known spiders. Their black-and-red abdomens warn other animals that they produce powerful venom.

Redback spiders usually live close to the ground. They bite people who get too close to their webs. Female redback spiders are more dangerous than the males because they are bigger. They have longer fangs, so they can inject more venom, and inject it more deeply.

Cinnabar Moths

Stunning cinnabar moths fly during the day. Their black-and-red wings warn predators that they are poisonous.

A cinnabar moth caterpillar feeds on ragwort leaves, which contain many poisons. As it eats, a cinnabar moth caterpillar stores the poisons in its body. The poisons stay in its body when it changes into a moth. This makes a cinnabar moth taste very bad to birds.

Vital Statistics

- **Wingspan:** up to 1.7 in (42 mm)
- **Habitat:** ragwort plants
- **Distribution:** Europe and Asia
- **Predators:** wasps and birds

A Cinnabar Moth's Black-and-Red Colors

A cinnabar moth's wings are jet black with bold red markings.

The bright colors of the black-and-red cinnabar moth warn predators that it is poisonous to eat.

15

Vital Statistics

- **Wingspan:** up to 3.5 in (88 mm)
- **Habitat:** milkweed plants
- **Distribution:** North, Central, and South America
- **Predators:** wasps and birds

A Queen Butterfly's Black-and-Orange Colors

The wings of a queen butterfly are orange with black veins and a black border. There are small white spots on the black border.

Queen Butterflies

Queen butterflies are large and colorful. Their black-and-orange wings send a message that they are poisonous to eat.

A queen butterfly caterpillar munches on poisonous milkweed plants. As it eats, it stores the poisons in its body. The poisons stay in its body, even when it changes into a butterfly. Any predator that tries to eat a queen butterfly gets very sick.

The poisonous queen butterfly has bright orange-and-black wings to warn predators away.

A black-and-orange gulf fritillary caterpillar tastes nasty to predators.

Vital Statistics

- **Wingspan of adult:** up to 3.7 in (95 mm)
- **Habitat:** passionflower vines
- **Distribution:** North, Central, and South America
- **Predators:** wasps and birds

Gulf Fritillaries

Striking gulf fritillaries are common visitors to gardens. Both caterpillar and adult gulf fritillaries have black-and-orange colors to warn predators that they are poisonous if eaten.

A gulf fritillary caterpillar eats only the leaves of some types of passionflower vines. The leaves contain poisons. Eating them makes a gulf fritillary caterpillar and an adult gulf fritillary poisonous to predators.

A Gulf Fritillary's Black-and-Orange Colors

A gulf fritillary caterpillar is orange with purple-gray stripes and long, black spines. The butterflies are orange with silver and black markings.

17

Giant Centipedes

A giant centipede has a pair of solid claws near its head. Its black-and-orange stripes warn predators that the claws are venomous.

A giant centipede has 15 to 191 pairs of legs and a pair of jawlike venomous claws. The centipede clamps the venomous claws firmly onto a predator when it is attacked. The tips of the claws puncture the predator's body and inject venom. The last pair of legs is used for fighting off predators.

Vital Statistics

- **Length:** up to 1 ft (30 cm)
- **Habitat:** rain forests
- **Distribution:** warm parts of the world
- **Predators:** toads, birds, badgers, and shrews

A Giant Centipede's Black-and-Orange Stripes

Some giant centipedes have bold black-and-orange stripes, and orange legs.

The venomous tiger centipede has black-and-orange stripes to warn predators that it is dangerous.

Honeybees

Honeybees sting other animals to defend themselves. Their black-and-orange stripes warn that they are dangerous.

Worker bees fly out and sting intruders when their nest is under threat. Each bee can sting only once, because it cannot pull its barbed stinger back out of the victim's flesh. It leaves the stinger in the victim and goes away to die. Muscles attached to the stinger keep pumping venom into the wound.

Vital Statistics

- **Length:** about 0.6 in (15 mm)
- **Habitat:** near flowers
- **Distribution:** almost worldwide
- **Predators:** other insects, spiders, frogs, and birds

A Honeybee's Black-and-Orange Stripes

Honeybees have black-and-orange, or black-and-dark-yellow stripes.

A black-and-orange striped honeybee can give predators a painful sting.

A poisonous fire salamander has bold black and yellow markings.

Vital Statistics

- **Length:** up to 1 ft (30 cm)
- **Habitat:** forests and woodlands
- **Distribution:** Europe
- **Predators:** snakes

A Fire Salamander's Black-and-Yellow Colors

A fire salamander is glossy black with bright yellow, or sometimes orange, markings.

Fire Salamanders

Shy fire salamanders spend most of their time hidden in damp places. Their black-and-yellow colors warn predators that they release poison.

A fire salamander releases a milky, poisonous liquid through tiny holes on its back if it feels threatened. It sprays the poison at the predator if it is about to be attacked. The poison irritates the skin and eyes of the predator and stops it from attacking the fire salamander.

Black-and-yellow colors warn that animals are likely to be poisonous or venomous.

Yellow-Bellied Sea Snakes

Yellow-bellied sea snakes are dangerous. Their vivid yellow bellies warn predators that they have venomous bites.

Yellow-bellied sea snakes swim or float near the ocean surface. They are **carnivores** that prey on fish. If yellow-bellied sea snakes are cornered, they sink their small fangs into predators and deliver their venom. If they get washed ashore they may bite humans who come too close.

Vital Statistics

- **Length:** 3.3 ft (1 m)
- **Habitat:** warm oceans
- **Distribution:** Indian and Pacific Oceans
- **Predators:** sharks

A Yellow-Bellied Sea Snake's Black-and-Yellow Colors

A yellow-bellied sea snake's back is black and its belly is yellow. Its tail is yellow with black spots or bars.

A yellow-bellied sea snake's yellow belly warns that the snake has powerful venom.

21

Black-and-Yellow Stripes...

Vital Statistics

- **Length:** 0.1 to 0.8 in (3 to 20 mm)
- **Habitat:** flowering plants and crops
- **Distribution:** almost worldwide
- **Predators:** other beetles, lizards, birds, shrews, and bats

Blister Beetles

Blister beetles defend themselves by releasing body fluids that cause blisters to form on a predator's skin. Some blister beetles have yellow stripes to warn other animals to stay away.

When an adult blister beetle is rubbed or pressed, it releases body fluids from its leg joints. The body fluids contain a substance that causes a predator's skin to blister. Some blister beetles release an oily substance that has a bad taste.

A Blister Beetle's Black-and-Yellow Stripes

Most blister beetles are black or gray but some have bright yellow stripes.

Black-and-yellow blister beetles can release harmful body fluids if attacked.

22

Black-and-yellow stripes can warn that animals have harmful body fluids or vicious stings.

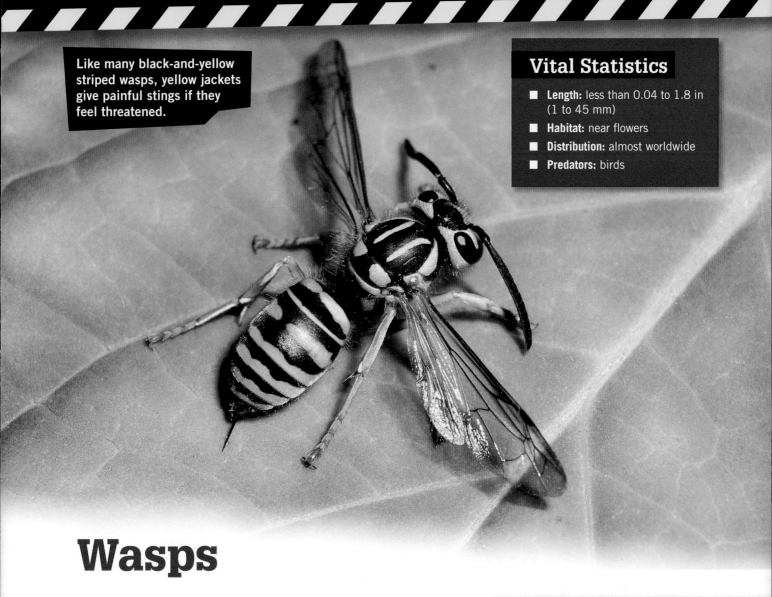

Like many black-and-yellow striped wasps, yellow jackets give painful stings if they feel threatened.

Vital Statistics

- **Length:** less than 0.04 to 1.8 in (1 to 45 mm)
- **Habitat:** near flowers
- **Distribution:** almost worldwide
- **Predators:** birds

Wasps

Some wasps sting to defend their nests and to **paralyze** their prey. Their black-and-yellow stripes warn other animals to keep their distance.

Many wasps are aggressive, and will attack intruders if their nests are disturbed. Each female wasp has a long, smooth sting. She can sting over and over again, because she can pull the sting back out of a victim's flesh. She injects venom into a wound each time she stings.

A Wasp's Black-and-Yellow Stripes

Most yellow jackets have black-and-yellow stripes. Some hornets, such as the Asian giant hornet, have black-and-yellow stripes as well.

Striped Skunks

A black-and-white striped skunk fires a smelly liquid when it is threatened.

Striped skunks are famous for their defense system. Their black-and-white colors warn other animals that they spray a foul-smelling liquid.

A striped skunk arches its back, raises its tail, and stamps its front feet to warn off a predator. If this warning is ignored, it fires a blast of stinking liquid at the predator. The liquid can cause temporary blindness and it has a horrible smell that is very difficult to remove from fur.

Vital Statistics

- **Length with tail:** 1.6 to 2.8 ft (49 to 86 cm)
- **Habitat:** open areas
- **Distribution:** North America
- **Predators:** owls, dogs, coyotes, foxes, and badgers

A Striped Skunk's Black-and-White Colors

A striped skunk is mostly black. It has two broad, white stripes on its back that join at the neck.

Striped Polecats

Striped polecats squirt a smelly liquid when they are in danger. Their black-and-white colors warn other animals to keep their distance.

A striped polecat growls, barks, and fluffs up its tail when it is annoyed by another animal. Then it lets out a shrill scream. It aims its bottom at the victim and squirts a foul-smelling liquid. The smell stays on the victim for days.

Vital Statistics

- **Length with tail:** 1.6 to 2.3 ft (50 to 70 cm)
- **Habitat:** forests, scrub, and grasslands
- **Distribution:** Africa
- **Predators:** dogs

A Striped Polecat's Black-and-White Colors

A striped polecat has glossy black fur. It has four broad, white stripes running from its head to its tail.

A black-and-white striped polecat squirts a foul-smelling liquid at predators.

25

A blue-ringed octopus's blue rings glow when the octopus is about to bite.

Vital Statistics

- **Armspan:** up to 5.9 in (15 cm)
- **Habitat:** rock pools and shallow water
- **Distribution:** Indian and Pacific Oceans
- **Predators:** fish, moray eels, and sharks

A Blue-Ringed Octopus's Blue Colors

Most of the time, a blue-ringed octopus is camouflaged to match its surroundings. It is only when a blue-ringed octopus is disturbed or provoked that its blue rings glow brightly.

Blue-Ringed Octopuses

Blue-ringed octopuses are among the most dangerous animals in the ocean. Their glowing blue rings warn that they have a venomous bite.

Blue-ringed octopuses lurk in rock crevices and rock pools. They display brilliant blue rings, spots, or lines when disturbed by predators. If predators do not move away after seeing this warning, blue-ringed octopuses bite. The bite is not very painful, but the venom acts quickly. It causes breathing difficulties and even death.

Poison Dart Frogs

Poison dart frogs are beautiful but extremely poisonous. Their spectacular blues and other colors warn predators "If you eat me, you will die!"

Tiny poison dart frogs look like jewels scattered throughout the rain forest. They ooze a powerful poison through their colorful skin when they are disturbed. Any predator that tries to eat a poison dart frog quickly spits it out because of the horrible taste. However, the predator will probably still die from the poison.

Vital Statistics

- **Length:** 0.4 to 2.4 in (1 to 6 cm)
- **Habitat:** rain forests
- **Distribution:** Central and South America
- **Predators:** snakes and birds

A Poison Dart Frog's Blue Colors

Poison dart frogs come in brilliant colors, including blue, blue and red, and blue, black, and yellow.

The poison dart frog has blue, black, and yellow colors to warn predators that it is poisonous.

Old World Swallowtail Caterpillars

Plump old world swallowtail caterpillars look more like eaters than fighters. However, their green, black, and orange colors warn that they can defend themselves by releasing a foul smell.

An old world swallowtail caterpillar munches on plants such as milk parsley, fennel, and wild carrot. It raises an orange, fork-shaped, fleshy organ from behind its head when it is alarmed. Then it releases a foul-smelling substance from the organ.

Vital Statistics

- **Wingspan of adult:** 3.1 to 3.9 in (8 to 10 cm)
- **Habitat:** milk parsley, fennel, and wild carrot plants
- **Distribution:** Europe, Asia, and North America
- **Predators:** ants, flies, and birds

An Old World Swallowtail Caterpillar's Green Colors

Young old world swallowtail caterpillars look similar to bird droppings. Older caterpillars are green, with small orange spots on narrow black bands.

The green, orange, and black old world swallowtail caterpillar can release a hideous smell to warn off predators.

Beautiful green-and-red shield bugs can release disgusting smells to warn off predators.

Shield Bugs

Shield bugs deter predators by releasing horrible smells. Their bright greens and other colors serve as a warning to predators to leave them alone.

A shield bug has special "stink" glands in its **thorax.** When it is disturbed, it releases a foul-smelling liquid through openings between its first and second pairs of legs. The smell is so bad that most predators want to get away as quickly as they can.

Vital Statistics

- **Length:** 0.2 to 0.4 in (5 to 10 mm)
- **Habitat:** crops and flowering plants
- **Distribution:** almost worldwide
- **Predators:** other bugs, lizards, and birds

A Shield Bug's Green Colors

Shield bugs come in all sorts of bright colors and patterns. Some have metallic green colors that gleam in the sunlight.

Double Defenses

Many animals have not just one, but two ways
to defend themselves from predators.

Ladybugs

Ladybugs come in a dazzling range of colors and patterns. They use warning colors and armor for protection.

A Ladybug's Warning Colors

Most ladybugs are yellow, orange, or red, with black markings. A ladybug's bright colors warn predators that it tastes nasty and may be poisonous. If a ladybug is handled roughly, it oozes a smelly yellow fluid from its leg joints.

A Ladybug's Armor

When a ladybug is not flying, its hard front wings meet in a straight line down the middle of its back. These hard front wings act as armor to protect the delicate flying wings and body underneath.

Glossary

abdomens	the last sections of the bodies of animals that don't have spines
allergic reactions	negative reactions in the body to some substances
carnivores	animals that eat meat
combined	put together
display	show
dorsal fin	the fin on the back of an animal
habitats	areas where animals live, feed, and breed
hind wings	the back pair of wings on an insect with two pairs of wings
inflate	blow up
paralyze	make unable to move
poisonous	contains poison
predators	animals that hunt and kill other animals for food
prey	animals that are hunted and caught for food by other animals
reputation	the way in which people regard someone or something
strikes	lunges forward and bites
thorax	the middle section of the body of animals without spines
venom	a type of poison
venomous	poisonous

Index